against the machine

AN EDUCATOR'S MEMOIR

ANDREA L. SUTTON, PH.D.

Copyright © 2017 by Dr. Andrea L. Sutton

All rights reserved.

Published in the United States by Drea & Drew Publishing, a division of Drea & Drew, LLC.

ISBN-13: 978-0998749211

ISBN-10: 0998749214

Edited by Janis Frazier

Cover photograph: Ricardo Navas

For my sons, Andrew and Andreas.
For my beloved parents, Marvin and Linda.
For dearest Mama Kate.
For the village that has supported me.
For my colleagues in the trenches who have found themselves without a voice.
For my Black and Brown children and their families who are counting on us.

"Do not be afraid or discouraged, for the Lord will personally go ahead of you.

He will be with you; He will never fail you nor abandon you."

Deuteronomy 31:8

Be the light.

CONTENTS

INTRODUCTION	**VI**
PART ONE: THE TRENCHES	**1**
REALITY CHECK	2
Templeton	4
Silence IS Deadly	20
"TRANSFORMING" EDUCATION	26
The Little Engine That Could	30
THE CHARTER GAMES	42
Good Intentions	42
First Grade	49
Loyalty	60
Dirty Laundry Money	67
Chartering False Hopes	77
PART TWO: THE MACHINE & ME	**81**
'ROUND WHERE I'M FROM	84
ABSENT A MENTOR	94
PART THREE: THE MACHINE	**98**
UNVEILED	99
A DREAM DEFERRED:	
EVERY CLOSED EYE AIN'T SLEEP	106
AFTERWORD	**124**
REFERENCES	**126**

INTRODUCTION

January 4, 2016

Dear Faculty and Staff,

When I accepted the position of Principal for Crooks Academy, I did so on the premise that I could use everything I've learned about curriculum and instruction, high-poverty urban schools, and the systematic exclusion of Black and Brown children from the higher ranks of society to craft a plan that would strategically enable and empower our students to succeed long after they leave us. I set out to ensure that our students would be provided the same educational opportunities that are extended to their wealthy counterparts in savvy private schools. This positon was personal for me. I was both spiritually and emotionally vested in the call to use my gifts to make a positive impact on the lives of children who came from the very community in which I grew up. It was an honor to lead that charge. Sadly, I came to realize that the ESPOUSED principles by which this organization operates are, indeed, diametrically opposed to its OPERATIONAL principles, thus undermining its stated mission. As G. Counts (1932) once warned, "we must beware lest we become so devoted to motion that we neglect the question of direction and be entirely satisfied with movement in circles." This organization is moving in circles and I'm dizzy.

Crooks is a company that is in the BUSINESS of education. It is a company that rewards loyalty over quality and mediocrity over excellence as long as the "bottom line" is preserved and maintained. This business mode of operation has handicapped our efforts. It is detrimental to our children and it is fundamentally in stark contrast to everything that I have come to believe about what is best for our children. That said, I am resigning from my position as Principal. I cannot, I will not, compromise my integrity by promoting the misappropriated, debilitating agenda of this company.

I wish you all the best in all that you endeavor to do.

Sincerely,

Dr. Sutton

This week is fairly open. I took my elder son to swim class yesterday evening, I'm taking them both to get haircuts today, and my little one has his swim class tomorrow. No meetings, only one cake to bake, just me and the boys and long overdue writing time. I've been going to the gym pretty much every day, except when we get a lot of snow---I hate the snow. I'm much better now you know. Mentally, physically, and spiritually. It's been a little less than one month since I resigned and, quite honestly, this is hands-down the makings of one of the greatest periods of my life. I have officially unplugged from the "matrix" and it feels AMAZING! As a person who has either been in school full-time, working full-time, or both at the same time for the past 16 years, finally, in this moment, I'm free.

I've been reflecting a great deal lately and, the more I reflect, the more lucidly this idea of what I call "the machine" has emerged. While this machine is not one physical object in the literal sense, it's theoretical basis and structural components manifest themselves in real tangible ways. This revelation has come about through what I candidly recognize as my own personal state of exhaustion. Exhaustion with the systems that I have been subjected to as a child and as an adult. This realization that I have centers around one simple question with profound and complex implications: Why is it that I have ALWAYS had to FIGHT for my Black and Brown students living in poverty? Quite frankly, education for "us" (arguably by design) is not and has never been equitable in terms of the opportunities, resources, and experiences that have been extended.

Together, we will explore this notion of the machine at work through a mere glimpse into my life. First, as a 25-year-old Ph.D. student at a local university in Miami, FL and a primary teacher at a high-poverty urban school in Miami-Dade County where I taught for 5 consecutive years. Next, as a senior high school teacher at a school targeted for "transformation" where I taught for one year before returning home to Ohio. I, then, taught for 2 years before working as a district consultant and later as a principal at a public charter school in Hamilton, Ohio. I share my experiences with you as a teacher, administrator, student, and parent. It is my hope that the exposure of those experiences will enlighten, inspire, and encourage those of us who are willing to continue fighting the good fight for all of God's children. Indeed, change is possible but it starts with us. My name is Dr. Sutton and this is my story.

PART ONE: THE TRENCHES

I want to welcome you to "the trenches." In the trenches, we are seldom given what we need to successfully educate our students. We are seldom supported by our district office or administrators. If it makes perfect sense, it likely doesn't happen here. If what you want to do or what you need requires financial resources, be prepared to reach in your own pocket and muster up whatever you can to get it. We are the home of the district leftovers and the land of lack. Our needs have never been a priority, even if overall student well-being depends on it. Here in the trenches, we make something out of nothing every… single… day.

-The High-Poverty Urban Public School Teacher in these United States of America

REALITY CHECK

Genesis elementary school was NOTHING like I'd ever seen before. I overheard horror stories from strangers about how off the chain the school was but I really didn't think it could be THAT bad. I should have known better when, in our first conversation, the principal was overwhelmed with excitement when she shared that video cameras were being installed that year. I just figured that, both she and the other people I spoke with were, like many folk, automatically fearful, nervous, and full of assumptions because the school was located in one of Miami's poorest neighborhoods. Up until the time I was in the fourth grade, I was raised in a community similar to the one that housed the school, so that was the least of my worries. In fact, that was the primary reason why I decided to accept my position there. I wanted to be where I felt I was needed the most.

When I walked into the school for the first time, (absent the barbed wire fence around the school and the eerie feeling that I was entering a prison) it didn't seem too bad. That is, until I saw my classroom. Honestly, my first reaction was "HELL. To. The NAW!" Everything in there was covered with a thick layer of dust and crud! It was literally the most disgusting room I had ever seen and it existed in a SCHOOL of all places! That just would not have happened in any school that I ever attended growing up, even if it was just a storage room where no children would ever be. Everything about it was completely unacceptable. Let's just say that I immediately understood how Ms. Celie must've felt when she walked into Mister's house for the first time in *The Color Purple*!

The mix-matched furniture was old and raggedy, the materials were old and raggedy, and everything in there looked like it came from off the street. The lighting was very poor and, even though one wall was consumed by windows, the handles to open the hurricane shutters were broken so I couldn't see out of them and light barely shined through. I simply could not believe how gross it was! The students were to report back to school in two days and I was expected to have my classroom together by then. Although I'd like to consider myself a fairly optimistic person, I really didn't know how I was going to pull that one off. Where I'm from, custodians clean and teachers teach. I quickly learned that at this school, if you want something done you have to do it yourself because no one was trying to help me clean that nasty room. Two days, rubber gloves, seemingly endless sneezing, surgical masks, some bleach (yes bleach), lots of praying, grace, surprises, screams, and one mysterious rash on my arm later, my classroom was finally transformed into the warm, welcoming, safe place for children that it should have been before.

Templeton

It was no secret that our school had rats but I had never seen one…that is, until this day. I was working with my children in a small reading group when out walked Templeton (for real, like the rat from *Charlotte's Web*)! That rat tiptoed across a utility pipe that connected the air conditioner to another part of the ceiling and my students hollered. Two of the five who were seated at the table with me darted towards the door. Immediately, I lined the children up with their backpacks and marched to the office. I brought in my entire class and sat them down. The principal was inside her office in a meeting so I was greeted by the assistant principal and the dialogue went like this:

AP: "What's the problem, Miss Sutton?"

Me: "A rat just came out in my classroom while I was working in a small group with my children."

AP: "Well, rats come out in my office and I still have to work so what's your excuse?"

Me: "Excuse me? You may be okay with working in an environment like that but I certainly am not nor do I have to and my children don't either. God forbid a rat bites one of my students! We are not going back into the classroom and we need to be placed somewhere else."

AP: "Go talk to your principal. She's in there in a meeting."

The conversation was beyond appalling to me. Perhaps the most shocking part about it was that it was coming from an assistant principal who was a new mother, and I thought she cared about our kids. Our rapport, however, had reminded me that she had simply been beaten down by the politics at our school and the system. She, like many of the veteran teachers, had a season or two where she tried to affect positive changes at our school on behalf of the children but metaphorically had the door slammed in her face so many times that she just lost hope.

The principal was having a meeting with the curriculum team in her office when I politely walked in and shared my concern. Her face expressed a look of great aggravation as if what I said wasn't of enough importance for me to have interrupted her meeting.

One of the curriculum team members sensed my rapidly developing anger and very quickly handed me her keys and suggested that I take the children to an empty classroom upstairs or into the cafeteria until dismissal. I thanked her and left. We spent the last forty minutes of the school day playing phonics games in the cafeteria. A small girl laid her head on my arm, peered up at me with sad eyes and whispered: "Thank you, Miss Sutton."

We were relocated to an upstairs classroom and, of course, rats were there too. Trails of red and blue crumbs were on a desk and inside the chair below were the remaining gnawed off crayons. We had been in the classroom for over a week and there still wasn't enough seating for my students. I had to rotate the children in groups, half seated with feet swinging under the tall raggedy desks and the other half seated on small multi-colored reading rugs that I brought up from my classroom. I was told that the custodians were going to put down some glue traps and we would be able to return in a few days but nothing ever happened. So, I decided to take matters into my own hands and make a call to the Health Department. It wasn't the first time they had heard from me. I had called once before after fighting off and killing fourteen flying roaches in my classroom last year. And, yes, I counted the number of roaches that I killed because after the sixth one I started getting EXTREMELY nervous. I had seen Palmetto bugs before but never enormous roaches with wings. YUCK!!! A sporadic three or four very large wingless roaches wandering out as if to join us with a lesson, that was typical. Spiders, lizards, and rat droppings, that was typical but, yeah, fourteen FLYING roaches was just too much. I didn't know whether to stay still, run, or duck! The health inspector was a short Cuban man. He went in, took notes, visited some other classrooms (including one next to me with a severe rat problem) and that was all we ever saw or heard from either him or the department. Nothing changed.

This time when I called, the Health Department sent a different inspector and boy was I happy to see that she was Black. My excitement was not due personal preference or bias but instead due to the undeniable observations that I'd made during my stay in Miami-Dade County which taught me that racism is, indeed, alive and well and that Cubans in positions of power have had a tendency to look out for the interests of their own. This school, with a population of more than 95% African-American and Haitian children, had the same Cuban principal when the first inspector came and the reports resulted in NO action at all. I mean I'm just saying. Maybe it was a coincidence. A happenstance of some sort? Just an observation.

It was clear, however, that the new health inspector was disturbed with what she saw. She went from class to class and in an out of miscellaneous rooms throughout the building taking pages of notes and listening to stories from teachers with unnerving experiences. One teacher had placed a Styrofoam takeout container with her left-over lunch in it on a table in her classroom while she attended a meeting during her planning time. She returned to find a huge rat with its head inside the container, eating the last of her lunch! During the time that my class was being held in the upstairs classroom, the rats had a field day in my room. One day, I had forgotten to lock my personal closet overnight and returned to find that the rats had eaten through my brand-new box of tampons (and you know I was hot because who was going to pay for it?!)! Cotton was sprawled on the shelf and remnants of chewed up cardboard and strings were loosely hanging inside the box. Had I not remembered that I left the closet unlocked I would've sworn we had super rats that broke through locks with their bare hands because the way that box and what used to be the contents of it was looking at that moment, anything was possible. These stories, among others, were shared with the inspector when she came. What she saw was confirmation enough that they were true. Her final report included not only our rat infestation but the moldy air ducts, broken water fountains, nonworking unsanitary restrooms, lack of soap, and unsanitary cafeteria as well. The school was given notification that the problems needed to be addressed immediately or the school could face closure.

The inspector had come back twice since her first visit. Each subsequent inspection yielded the same unsatisfactory rating. The children and I had since been settled back into the "rat room" after three glue traps were so-called strategically placed in attempt to capture our four-legged students. At that point, no major attempts had been made to address the infestation of the school. Thus, one of my students (go figure) had the pleasure of meeting Templeton's cousin in the cafeteria. She returned from lunch highly distraught because, while she was eating, a rat stood on her shoe and she stepped on its tail when trying to shew it away! That said, her mother was outraged. Yet, all she got was "The Great Runaround" from the school administration and the district. All the actors involved in the hierarchal process made sure the voices of OUR parents and concerned teachers were never heard by folk who would do something about it! Even when calling the Superintendent's office, it seemed as though those who were directly around him conveniently neglected to relay any messages.

The media soon became the only viable outlet, but it was difficult to find a newspaper or news station that was willing to run the story. Then, I remembered a random conversation that I once had with one of my mentor teachers who had recently retired. She had told me about a reporter for the Miami Herald who had once conducted research regarding schooling issues and had not too long ago revealed some kind of scandal in another school in Miami-Dade County. I got the man's name and called him up myself. He told me that I wasn't the first teacher to reach out for help. There were others that had gone before me, not only from my school over the years but from others in the county. Nothing had ever come of their stories because all were too terrified to reveal themselves as sources of the information, and such strong accusations required credibility that could only be established by someone on the inside. I, on the other hand, was fearless when it came to demanding justice for our children. I wasn't worried about protecting myself or my job in this case because I am a woman of faith and I strongly believe that when your heart is in the right place, when you risk all to advocate for those who cannot advocate for themselves, the children in this case, God will not only fight for you but He will also secure your position or bless you with one that is greater. It had to be done and I was more than willing.

I met with him down the street from my school on my lunch break. I disclosed the information and outcomes pertaining to the recent reports from the Health Department among other issues at our school while he took notes. That same night I spoke with a close friend of mine who was well seasoned pertaining to the politics of Miami and, without hesitation, he warned me not to give consent for my name to be revealed. He was concerned that it was too early in my career to risk being relocated and "black-balled", and that I would no longer be able to be there for my students if that happened. It was with that perspective that I changed my mind and called to retract my permission. The very next morning, a new window of opportunity opened. I shared what happened with an angry parent who was eager to go forward on behalf of everyone, and so she did. Things fell immediately into place without me having to position myself directly in the midst of the oncoming traffic.

Our story hit the news that next day! While on my way to work that morning, I stopped at a gas station to get coffee. As I was waiting in line to pay, my eyes casually swept across my immediate surroundings for entertainment and boy was I in for it! A headline from the front page of the Miami Herald screamed from the newsstand: *"Rats Freely Roam Miami School: Dashing in and Out of Classrooms, Rats Have Invaded Genesis Elementary School in Miami."* At that moment, so many emotions simultaneously erupted inside of me. Feelings of great joy, amazement, and relief walked hand in hand with anxiousness, disappointment, and shame. I was happy and relieved because of my hope that maybe now things would get better. Such bad publicity for us was like the fire under the pot that would finally cause the water to boil. The anxiousness, disappointment, and shame stemmed from the uncertainty in not knowing what the outcome would be, paired with the disgrace that our situation was so bad that it had come to that point.

As I approached the school, the realization of what was happening was solidified with the news vans that were parked out front and the inquiring reporters who stood alongside of them. As I slowly pulled into the parking lot, I spotted the reporter that I spoke with. We made eye contact and each gave a subtle nod, discreetly acknowledging the presence of each other while at the same time acting as total strangers. I learned very quickly how to become one of the Oscar-winning actresses, how to fake a surprised face and speak as if I knew nothing at all about what was going on. My performance successfully confused administration and other teachers who were sent to spy for the principal while she played invisible woman in her office all day (not as if she was visible around the school any other time but she refused to answer calls or open her door). There was vast speculation, but no one could quite put their finger on it and I wasn't about to let them know.

My students, like most 6 and 7-year-old's, entered the classroom and walked straight to the window to stare at the strangers in weird vans with metal straws on top and those outside holding microphones and video cameras. Some of them had already heard the news while others didn't have a clue what was happening. I told them that the people who were outside were here to help us get rid of the rats and clean our school up. One child's response alone was worth more than any risks involved: "Thank, God. It's about time somebody cleaned this place up. We're gonna be okay now, Miss Sutton," he said with confidence and a blushing grin on his face. That comment from my six-year-old student let me know that, although I had never explicitly told them that I was fighting for them, they knew it. They had been there the whole time quietly observing the interactions between myself and other staff, the inspectors, administration, custodians, and parents. If they didn't understand anything else, they were well aware of my love for them. The love that allowed me to care for them as I would my own even if I had to sacrifice my own career to do so. That moment is something that I will never forget.

> ### A Voice from the Trenches
> "It got to the point where the rats were literally taking over our building. That year, I was teaching Kindergarten and we had the big crayons. For some reason, the rats loved the red ones. We would come in Monday mornings and all the red crayons would be chewed up. At that time, we didn't have whiteboards, we had chalkboards and all over our desks you would see footprints from where the rats had been in the chalk dust on the chalkboard ledge and then all around the

room. You would see footprints of, not mice, rats all around the room so we knew they were there. I was the type that, if I didn't see them during the day, I was fine. This one wooden cabinet in my room was old and raggedy and it had holes chewed in it. I guess that's where they were living. We would keep our art supplies in there--the newsprint, and construction paper. Well, they were making nests and we didn't see it. One day, I was with my kids and had opened the cabinet to get some construction paper and a whole bunch of baby rats jumped out at me! All I could do was scream and run down the hallway like a crazy person! It was just chaos! The kids were running around and rats were running everywhere and all my principal could say was "shut the door until we can get someone to come in and clean the room". So, we were out of the room for about two weeks because we couldn't get anyone to come in and kill all the rats.

I was at that school for 11 years, I taught 6 years in kindergarten and the rest in 4th grade and it was the best experience I've ever had. The teaching and my students. I've worked with kids who other teachers just really couldn't tolerate, so they just moved them out and put them in my class and they ended up being some of the highest achieving students I ever had. Some of those students call me now just to keep me abreast of what they are doing, what they majored in, and what job they got. All of that was sort of worth it. Even if it's just 5 kids. One little girl was in this other teacher's class and, I hate to say this, but she was very prejudiced and had problems working with students of other ethnicities. This teacher would insult the kids but this little girl was very stubborn and she refused to allow her to treat her any kind of way so, of course, they bumped heads. It got to the point where if they didn't pull her out, she probably would have been sent to the juvenile detention center, because I could just see her getting that upset. She was moved into my class. When I got her, all I had heard were bad reports but, of course, that changed. That little girl is now an electrical engineer, and she moved out of state and is doing wonderful. As rough and tough as it got at that school, I really had some great days. The kids had to work through a lot. I still have gifts that students gave me and you can tell it was probably soap from their mother's bathroom, but I cherished that because they didn't have anything and they wanted to give me something."

Silence IS Deadly

For years, we were invisible. We must've been invisible. It was as though no one saw or heard us at all. Everything from the old barbed-wire fence surrounding the school building to the inside that was plagued by poor lighting, leaking ceilings, broken air conditioners, unusable restrooms and drinking fountains, exposed wire, and holes in the walls and ceilings, and moldy air ducts said it had to be so. Our floors were waxed and cleaned once a year or not at all. Toilet paper and soap were strangers in our restrooms. Many of our classrooms lacked enough seats, tables, and/or desks for our students and most of the ones we did have were old, raggedy, and in some cases, dangerous to occupy. Basic supplies like primary writing paper and pencils were rarely provided. Need I mention the rats again? Actual rats! In some classrooms, rats were greeted daily by students who were instructed by their teachers to adhere to the "rat rules" and not bother them. It was no secret that the rats would run back and forth across the cafeteria stage and through the lines of children who were waiting for their food. At a school where nearly 95% qualify, students whose parents had not yet completed a renewal application for free/reduced lunch were given four saltine crackers and a slice of cheese for lunch to sustain them until our 4:00 dismissal. Students were permitted to run the halls, curse and hit each other and their teachers, and do whatsoever they pleased with little to no consequences for their actions.

For close to one year of semi-silent observation, I kept asking myself why such conditions were permitted to exist. I had heard about schools like this one but I had never seen or experienced life inside walls such as this. The more I began to ask questions, the more I began to realize that the manifestation of such horrible conditions were simply a reflection of both the principal's beliefs about the children of whom she served as well as the beliefs of the school district. Perhaps if our students were viewed as children who were perfectly capable of exhibiting positive behaviors in a school setting, they would have been taught how to do so instead of being permitted to conduct themselves as they saw fit. Perhaps if our students were viewed as human beings who, like us, desire and deserve to come to school in a clean, safe environment, the building would not have been in such poor condition and the rats and roaches would not have outgrown the student population. Perhaps if our students were viewed as children who are capable of learning and excelling academically, the school culture and environment would have been set up for their success, not for their failure.

Due to the negative attention from the media that our school received, additional schools had since received "unsatisfactory" ratings from the Health Department for similar issues. While it was sad to know that children from other schools in other communities were victims of the same type of neglect, I was delighted to know that at least now they too may have a shot at justice for their situation. I wondered about their teachers. Were they as afraid to speak up and out against it as ours had been? Did they try and no one listened? Or were they, like many others, suffering from a mentality of defeat or the apparent sheer lack of concern that trickled down from the top?

Some of our teachers expressed that they found it increasingly more difficult to fight on behalf of students once they had developed a perception that the parents don't care. While some parents may have legitimate reasons why they're never present, such as long work hours or the lack of leave time from low-level jobs (socioeconomic status and low wages play into this aspect significantly—which is part of the reason why high-poverty urban schools seem to be stricken with lack of parental involvement and support more often than others), there exists a group of parents (of whom we often make excuses for) who are in fact uninterested when it comes to anything having to do with their child's education. What we fail to consider, however, is the group of parents who (although concerned) just don't know how or where to begin when navigating the system. Perhaps they feel bound by their own inadequacies or harbor their own bad experiences with school which makes them too uncomfortable to come around? Or, perhaps they too attended the same school or one with conditions that mirror what they see at their child's designated school so they are simply unaware that they should expect and demand something different? Nevertheless, schools like Genesis are notorious for the lack of parental support they receive. Parent-teacher conference nights became teacher social hours or additional planning time because our parents simply did not show up (except for one or two). The difference between schools like Genesis and schools who provide outstanding services and facilities for their students is not wholly the additional outside funding they may/may not receive; the active presence of parents undoubtedly serves as one determining factor. Yet, while we have no control over the lives of our students when they come to us nor a say in what goes on when they leave us, it is my belief that they are OUR children while they are in our classrooms and every adult in the building has a moral and ethical responsibility to secure their safety, even if it means that we must fight for it.

"TRANSFORMING" EDUCATION

"Like a baby shaking a rattle, we seem to be utterly content with action, provided it is sufficiently rigorous and noisy."

G. Counts (1932)

After the birth of my eldest son, I decided to take a break from elementary school instruction and transition to high school. I was already certified in Reading K-12, so that made my transition much more feasible. I accepted a position teaching 9 & 10th grade Intensive Reading at a senior high school. During this time, I had recently completed my comprehensive exams and was entering the dissertation phase of my Ph.D. program. While I went back and forth contemplating exactly how I would go about it, I knew that I wanted my dissertation to highlight the voices of teachers in the trenches.

As a teacher, I often felt like my own voice was silenced and it all seemed illogical to me. At a district-level, how can you make beneficial decisions about curriculum and instruction in schools when you have yet to inquire about curriculum and instructional application in schools from those who are on the front lines charged with delivering and facilitating instruction in those schools? In my humble opinion [insert a reasonable amount of sarcasm here], walking through a building spending 3-5 minutes (if that) in a couple of classrooms and then drawing one's own conclusions based upon limited knowledge and observations is simply insufficient when using it to make decisions of that magnitude. With Race to the Top on the rise and the subsequent formation of Miami-Dade County Public Schools' (M-DCPS) Education Transformation Office (ETO) and Education Transformation (ET) Schools, I decided to investigate teacher perceptions of education reform mandates in high-poverty urban schools.

In accordance with the State of Florida's new requirements for turning around the state's lowest-achieving schools, M-DCPS (2010) developed a comprehensive plan to "improve student achievement outcomes and increase high school graduation rates by focusing on extended learning opportunities, providing intensive student interventions based on assessment data, and offering job-embedded professional development and financial incentives to teachers". As a result, the district received 14 million dollars over three years through Florida's School Improvement Grant (SIG) to assist with implementation of the reform plan. The district's 19 lowest-achieving schools, known as ET schools, were targeted for turnaround making them contractually required to adhere to specific guidelines regarding highly qualified instructional staff, increased rigor, curriculum alignment and pacing, assessment, job-embedded professional development, extending learning opportunities, financial incentives for teachers, and parent/teacher conferences. Sounds great, right? Both my new school and my old school were among those listed.

My dissertation research became centered around the 19 ET schools and how teachers in those schools perceived the policy that dictated how they were to teach as well as the way curricula and resources were to be organized and utilized around the goal of improving their schools. I also investigated the role that school context (both individual school context and the high-poverty urban school context in general) played in determining their perceptions. Mandated accountability and assessment policies grounded in standardization had become embedded components of public schools in attempt to improve a "failing system" and ensure that all students had access to a quality education and the ET mandates were certainly no exception.

The top-down nature of those types of reform efforts, however, is often problematic because it precludes consideration for contextual factors at the local level, leading to different outcomes across schools. Previous researchers have concluded that policies in and of themselves do not inherently determine policy outcomes; rather, outcomes depend upon the interactions between the policy, the people who matter to its implementation, and the conditions in which they operate (Honig, 2009). This emphasis on accountability reform mandates for failing high-poverty urban schools that demand increased standardization and attaches incredibly high-stakes for non-compliance suggests a one-size-fits-all remedy for improvement that denies consideration of contextual factors and, subsequently, silences the voices of teachers (Ayers, et. al 2009). Since teachers are both the primary means by which curricula are implemented and direct witnesses of implementation outcomes, their feedback remains critical for providing firsthand insight about how these reforms impact students. I hoped to shed some light in that regard.

The Little Engine That Could

Given the context within which they work, most teachers felt as though the mandates were unrealistic and impractical. They frequently held negative perceptions of ETO staff, repeatedly noted persistent disorganization with ETO and their respective schools, and often referred to what they perceived as an unsupportive environment in which they work. Teachers indicated that their work had, indeed, become standardized and that oftentimes they had resorted to giving superficial performances in effort to appear as though they were complying with ETO demands. Due to the imposed mandates and the way they were managed at their respective locations, most teachers indicated grappling with persistent anxiety and frustration and expressed serious concerns about the impact of excessive testing on their students. While most teachers were required to implement the curriculum with fidelity, have identical lesson planning documents, and teach the same content at the same time as other colleagues who teach the same grade level and content area, the teachers felt that uniform implementation of the curriculum was seldom or never effective at meeting the needs of their students. That finding was consistent with Darling-Hammond's (1997) claim that there are no prepackaged sets of lessons or steps that ensure understanding for all learners in the same manner. She argued that successful teachers must be able to create experiences that make ideas accessible in a variety of ways of which always press for deep disciplined understanding. Teachers in ET schools didn't have that kind of freedom. Venturing off script for any reason was prohibited by the ET mandate which required standardization and fidelity to program implementation to the extent that differentiation of instruction in that regard was forbidden.

A Voice from the Trenches

"At my old school, we had so much freedom but now here I am, on the plantation. Literally. I feel like I am a slave on the plantation at work. I cannot for two seconds deviate from the script because it would be an issue. I feel like I have no freedom because I am suffocating from all of the to-dos at my job. I came from an 'A' school where we didn't do all of this. All this extra. I call it fluff. There's so much fluff. I call it smoke and mirrors because when you come in you're like, "wow". The data doesn't reflect all of this. You come in and everything is painted and there are pictures all around, but if you look closely, the pictures say 2007. We're not in 2007 anymore, so you're pushing this perception of what we are that's not even current. They come in your room, "Put more things on your wall, you need to have print rich environment." That's not what print rich means. It doesn't mean I buy more posters and plaster them all over my classroom and literally cover every single inch from top to bottom. Research actually shows that is a distraction, not a support for learning. I came from an A school, we don't focus on this right here. Binders, data boards, data walls, agenda all over your board with learning targets written, focus wall…my board is full of stuff that just needs to stay on there for them, not for us. There are too many parts that you have to tend to that you spend so much time trying to tend to the parts, making sure you are checking them off your list, that you don't have time to focus on the work of teaching. What happens is you end up frustrated. Like, "Yall better hurry up, you're taking too long", because you're looking at the clock and you know they need to finish this test because you have to submit the report by a certain time and it's just too much."

Based on the data from my study, it can be said that teachers perceive context as a factor whose consideration is critical to understanding how to effectively tailor instruction to meet the needs of their students. They felt that mandated uniformity, regarding the planning and implementation of curriculum, was unrealistic and impractical within the context of their classrooms and their schools. As one teacher clearly described: "They have about 10 high schools and not all of them are the same and I think they're holding everyone to the same level and that has been a great hindrance to our school…I feel like I'm not being able to address the needs of my students because they're asking me to do something else." Many of them felt there was genuinely a disconnect between ETO staff (the people who were sent from the district to check to provide implementation support and make sure they were following orders) and the realities of the school and their classrooms.

Teachers also reported that their suggestions and concerns were often silenced and seldom entertained. As demonstrated by the reported unwillingness to consider teacher feedback about the implementation process and how it was impacting students, results of the study suggested that the ETO was not at all concerned about individual school and classroom context; their only concern was making sure teachers were sticking to the district prescribed plan. Hence, teachers perceived ETO staff as more of a hindrance to instruction than as an immediate source of instructional support.

> ### A Voice from the Trenches
>
> "I truly believe that the goals of the Education Transformation Office are to move our school forward. I believe that is what they want to do but the way they are going about it is not working. I use this analogy when thinking about it: There's a room that needs to be painted and someone is taking paint and just splashing it everywhere and they're trying to paint this room. I think that they're doing it in a way that it lacks strategy. It lacks organization. It lacks support. It's hit or miss. They're just randomly trying to figure out how to do this and they're doing it almost blindly. I do believe they want to push the school forward. I believe they want to show that their system works. I believe that they have the same goal that we have but they really need to work on their methodology for reaching it."

M-DCPS, like countless other districts across the country, was seemingly "head over heels" for testing. The purpose for administering so many assessments was to provide teachers with data to guide instruction and interventions for students as indicated by the mandate. However, the results from the study revealed that, in practice, excessive testing diminished the intended usefulness of the data. Although most teachers in the ET schools agreed that assessment data in general was useful for guiding instruction, nearly half of them reported that their data was rarely helpful because their students were tested too much (especially high school teachers). This finding is consistent with findings from other researchers who concluded that while teachers in their study agreed with the overall concept of a policy which primarily required them to use data to drive instruction, under the current conditions, effective implementation appeared unrealistic to them (Ingram, Louis, & Schroeder, 2004). In other words, there was a mismatch between what they had actually experienced in their classrooms and what the theory behind the accountability system had assumed it would be.

Findings from the study suggested that mandating the standardization of curriculum and instruction in high-poverty urban schools is simply not the most effective means for ensuring that the needs of students in such schools will be met. To accommodate the needs of their students, teachers must be permitted to retain some level of autonomy as it pertains to instructional decision making in their classrooms. At a district level, in effort to obtain information that more accurately reflects classroom instruction, multiple opportunities must be provided for more thorough observation that is not divorced from teacher input or consideration for contextual factors. Hence, teachers may not perceive district feedback and subsequent demands as disconnected hindrances to their ability to effectively teach their students, thus, encouraging the implementation of improved curriculum and instruction efforts in high-poverty urban schools.

These findings raised significant questions for me: Is it not the responsibility of every teacher to ensure they are meeting the needs of all learners in their classrooms? If teachers viewed these policies as unrealistic and impractical within the context of their classrooms and their schools, why should it be expected that they comply? Should teachers not serve as advocates for their students? Evidence from the study provides support for Payne's (2010) argument that more time needs to be spent asking those working inside the walls of the schools about the internal problems of those schools and seeking solutions together rather than simply dictating orders from outside. This "decontextualized thinking" (Payne, p.62), as demonstrated by the apparent unwillingness to listen to teachers and the reluctance to thoughtfully consider contextual influences when making reform demands, impedes substantive change. These schools that are struggling, these schools that are positioned for "transformation" efforts, yet again, are schools that serve predominately Black and Brown children. Common approaches to transforming these schools create the appearance of superficial gains at best, while, at the same time, exacerbating the underlying difficulties they face. To truly educate is to empower. I'm left to question the overall intent.

> ### A Voice from the Trenches
>
> "I think one of my biggest frustrations is when somebody like your Assistant Principal comes in and he's running a meeting with the Language Arts department and he says, "Ok, ETO's coming next week" and he has a full page of what we have to have and what we better show. We better show all these things because that's what they expect us to show. I have to print everything out from the printer in my classroom because the Xerox machine hasn't worked at my school for over 3 months. The state says there should be only 15 kids in a classroom but I've got over 25. I can't get copies and my classes are overcrowded, and I have all these things that I HAVE to do. But, the things that you guys are supposed to do, you don't have to do them. What it felt like was, and I understand this completely, even if you're not really doing it, make sure you're faking it really well. I have a notebook of my colored charts and my everything in there with my kids from FAIR boxed and my little pie charts printed out because I know if I do that they'll leave me alone. If this is ETO's tool for transformation, if the effect of it is

> to make everybody fake what they are asking for just to get them off their backs because what they're asking you to do isn't helping actual students anyway (it's really pulling you away from time you could be spending planning thoughtful and engaging lessons for your students), then what have you accomplished exactly?"

THE CHARTER GAMES

Good Intentions

I had never considered becoming a principal before. It just wasn't something that I was interested in. I had devoted a significant amount of time and energy to my work and I knew that taking on the weight of a principal or an assistant principal role would require much more than I could give as a single parent with two small children at home. Plus, after nine years in the classroom and one year as a district consultant, I had developed what I'd like to call system fatigue. System fatigue is different from teacher burnout. As the name implies, it is educator exhaustion resulting from bureaucratic pressure and the tension it yields when trying to uphold institutional demands within a context that, quite frankly, it doesn't make sense to. Assuming the role of principal, in my mind, would only exacerbate the problem.

One day an unexpected opportunity presented itself. The principal at my son's school (who had been a close family friend for all my life) revealed to me that she was planning to move in another direction with her career and she would only feel comfortable doing so if I became principal in her stead. I had a "wait, what?" moment real quick! After all, I had just stopped by the school to let her know that I didn't intend to reenroll Drew for the next school year; I wasn't ready for all of that! In fact, my initial response (for reasons previously described) was, "umm…thank you but no! I can find someone for you though!" She refused to accept that answer. She told me she would give me two weeks to think about it and change my mind before she submitted my name as her recommendation anyway.

I tossed the idea around in my head during the weeks that followed. I prayed on it, that God would align my heart and my mind according to His will for my next steps. I thought about the children and their families there who were growing up in the same poor neighborhood where I was raised, subjected to the same subtle biases that I experienced in our city's schools, facing the same educational roadblocks that they will need to know how to strategically overcome. I thought about the nonprofit work that I was already doing within the community, as a mentor and educational advocate. I had begun to see the role of principal as what could be my ministry outside of the church walls. It was an opportunity for me to use everything that I've learned to give back, to empower children and their families to be able overcome the inevitable challenges ahead. The initial reservations and doubts that I held about taking the job soon turned into feelings of excitement about the possibilities and perceived opportunities to affect real change. I accepted the position.

For the next several weeks, I kept quiet about my decision. At that point, nobody knew that the current principal was leaving and she wanted to keep it that way until the school year ended so I decided used that to my advantage. I developed a teacher questionnaire in an effort to gain some insight about the school outside of the views shared from "the top". After all, I had to put that dissertation data to some use, right? The teachers were asked to provide their input regarding: Instruction, Professional Development, Building Procedures & Routines, Resources, and Job Satisfaction. Their feedback was then used to inform my planning for the upcoming year. Only 5 of those faculty members returned for the next school year. Nine new teachers would be joining them and, of those, 6 would be first year teachers.

    Less than a week after my contract ended at my previous job, I started my work as principal. I walked through the building and immediately began assessing resources at our disposal, resources that I knew we would need to be successful, and what we could do to spruce up the old building. I was the new kid on the block and the owners, at that time, wanted to make a good impression. I used that to land us some colorful paint for the doors and the entryway. I brought books from home and found bags of old books in a storage closet that I placed along the stage in the cafeteria so that students could grab a book to read or peruse while waiting after breakfast or during lunch. I had envisioned a collegial atmosphere built on mutual respect for one another and a spirit of excellence in the building. I wanted our students and their families to feel welcomed, to experience a sense of wonder and inspiration when entering the building. The new art teacher volunteered to paint a large mural in the stairwell and soon, the hallways would be filled with student work.

I was so excited about my plans for the upcoming school year to the extent that it often kept me up at night, strategizing and organizing ideas. I had a clear, overarching agenda and that was to empower and inspire our students and their families. Everything that was to be done this year would be centered around a building-wide initiative I dubbed "The Black & Brown Project". The overall goal of the Black & Brown Project was to increase student self-confidence by countering the popular negative narratives surrounding people of color and encouraging all students to strive hard to reach their goals because, indeed, anything is possible. Roughly 98% of our student body was Black or Brown and they needed to (on a regular basis) see people who look like them embodying the very things they might aspire to be. They wouldn't get to experience that in our city's public schools were the majority of the student population is White, the teachers are White, the curriculum and books are White-washed, and a standard White worldview dictates their potential. This project would involve short and long term goal setting, weekly immersion in Black and Brown history, and monthly "Meet a Professional" encounters so that students could learn about the person, the trade, and their experience. It would also serve as a lens through which teachers would view their everyday instruction. We would incorporate job-embedded professional development around the initiative along with ways to infuse it with our project-based learning efforts. At least, that was the plan anyway.

I thought about the private school that my son was initially going to attend that year. Students in all grades received Spanish instruction from a native Spanish speaker, Problem-solving Lab time was built into their weekly schedules, and it had a strong collaborative, collegial feel to it. I wanted to create that for Crooks Academy students but I had to do it strategically because our school was a public charter with "limited" funds, not a private, tuition-based institution. I had to hire an English Language Learner Specialist anyway, so I prayed for one who could teach Spanish and a way to be able to work it into her schedule without pulling her away from her primary assignment. I needed to hire a building substitute, so I hired a former Project-based Learning consultant to lead that effort in our building as our official Project-based Learning Coordinator. She would also serve as a substitute as needed. I was permitted to hire a Computer Science instructor, which I knew would be a tremendous asset for our students. I restructured schedules to make them more efficient so students would have enough time for core area instruction and remediation and so that teachers would be able to utilize common planning times for more effective collaboration efforts or grade-level professional development as needed. But, as the saying goes, "The best laid plans of mice and men often go awry".

First Grade

We had two first grade classes that year. My son, Drew, was in one of them. He had a first-year teacher who, despite the struggles that come along with being a first-year teacher, I was confident could get the job done. She knew her content, it was clear that she was passionate about teaching, and she went out of her way to make sure that her students had authentic learning experiences. The other first grade class, however, experienced turbulence from the very beginning. Due to limited access and exposure to quality educators, I found myself in a position where I was forced to start the school year without another first-grade teacher. Since our new Project-based Learning Coordinator, Ms. P, was also our building sub designee, by default (instead of working toward building out our school-wide initiative from the start of the year as I had intended) she had to assume the role of first grade teacher until I could hire a qualified candidate. I remember telling her the day before Open House that I needed her to temporarily serve in the new role and in one day she had transformed the empty room into a warm and inviting space for her incoming students.

    I was eager to find a permanent teacher for that class. Staffing had been extremely challenging for me during the summer. I would get several applications or resumes from district office from which I was to sift through and call in potential candidates for interviews. This procedure was problematic for me in that the other principals in our district were in desperate need of teachers as well so I, leading the only school in our district outside of the city where the main campuses were located, oftentimes would get the leftover applicants that nobody else wanted to hire, or I would receive the applications so late that they had already accepted positions elsewhere. In addition, I learned that our district didn't want to pay the fees associated with joining local job consortiums (one stop applicant hubs where teachers and other potential staff members could submit an application to be considered for employment in all of the local school district members of that particular consortium). This meant that our applicant pool was solely comprised of teachers who had applied directly to our school district which, when compared to surrounding districts, was too little known and far too small to compete. As a relatively small charter organization with little publicity outside of the city where the other campuses were located, this was not a good thing. It meant that quality candidates were out there looking for jobs that I could provide but I didn't have access to them because they were unaware that our school existed. Our reputation wasn't exactly the greatest either so, more often than not, those who did apply weren't always the candidates you'd love to hire.

Trying to staff our building was by far one of the most grueling, unpredictable processes that I had to endure. The other principals struggled immensely with the same task. In fact, it was so bad that we had to push back the start of our school calendar year at the last minute in effort to allow more time for us to find teachers to cover our classes. The entire calendar for the school year was pushed back just weeks before the school was expected to begin. That's absurd. Eventually, after two months of us principals griping about the staffing struggle while pointing to our classes beginning the year with substitutes, the owner finally agreed to pay the money and join the consortium.

By the fifth week of school, I had hired another first grade teacher and, at that stage in the game, you could only imagine how that worked out. Ms. P, whose previous experience in education was with intermediate students and not primary students, had worked hard to establish routines and maintain a classroom environment in which the first graders could thrive and have a successful year, but it did not come without its own challenges. This particular class had a high percentage of students who struggled with undiagnosed emotional and behavioral issues, but the overall class size was low (unlike the other first grade class), so it made classroom management a little easier to manage and support. I later learned that these same students had struggled with their behaviors in Kindergarten as well. As a principal, one logical response may have been to swap students from the other first grade class in effort to balance the behaviors but, although I moved several out of the more challenging class to the other class, I was reluctant to move any in. Classroom routines had already been established and the students in the other class were doing well. It wasn't enough for me to justify shifting students from a stable environment with a great teacher to an unstable environment with a teacher whose performance was yet to be determined.

Nevertheless, we worked together to make the teacher transition as smooth as possible for the children and their parents alike. The new teacher was to observe and work alongside Ms. P for the first week and slowly transition in by the end of the week. Since Ms. P wasn't actually leaving the building, it made things a little bit easier, especially for her students who had become particularly attached. The first several days the new teacher was in the building, I was away but nearby at a required training. I received daily updates regarding class progress and it appeared, at least in the very beginning, that it was going to be okay but boy did that take a turn for the worst! After my first week back in the building making my rounds of observations, I was begging for a "do over", literally! This woman was so nonchalant about EVERYTHING that it made me nervous. Though she had no children of her own, she reminded me of that exhausted parent that completely tunes the kids out while chaos is erupting all around the house! This woman had ZERO classroom management and she surely didn't stand a chance with that class!

By the time I was permitted to terminate her, roughly 2 months had passed. The behaviors in the class had escalated to crayons and other objects regularly being thrown, children screaming and talking back to the teacher, and running around the classroom in a complete free for all. As you might assume, there was little to no learning taking place at all. As principal, I was in that classroom every day putting out fires and/or trying to show my face in effort to prevent the next tragedy. I tried sharing and modeling classroom management, engagement, and teaching strategies. I tried rotating other teachers through there to give her some extra support. You name it. I tried it. Nothing worked. It was impossible for me to be in there all day every day to manage the class, teach the class and run the building at the same time, not effectively anyway. What was worse, she maintained the same nonchalant disposition through it all and her students were not learning. With 9 new teachers to manage and 5 returning teachers (with attitude) on top of that first grade class, you could imagine my struggle at that point.

That said, we ended up back at square one with Ms. P in the class until I could find them another teacher. It took, yet again, another several weeks just to get them back into a routine of learning and, quite frankly, the damage had already been done. Behavior problems had become the norm in that classroom, learning came second to classroom management, and many students had fallen significantly behind. On top of that, the grades that had been entered by the previous teacher were few and they appeared to be inflated at best. Ms. P administered some informal assessments to see just how far behind they were. Her lessons that followed attempted to target those weaknesses and students had additional opportunities to accumulate more grades that were more reflective of their actual learning progress. The new grades were slightly weighted in the system so that they would have more bearing once they were added to the previous inflated grades. Once the new grades were entered into the electronic gradebook, the students' overall grades plummeted. While I was disappointed that they were so low, it didn't take me by too much of a surprise considering the fact that their instruction had been limited significantly due to the classroom climate.

Although I certainly wasn't looking forward to the upcoming discussions with parents during conferences, they most definitely needed to know what was going on and I was prepared to take the heat. Then the unexpected happened. When word got back to the Superintendent that the grades were low in that class, this woman actually went into the system, removed the weights that their teacher had applied to the assignments and changed the grades to bring them up. Then, I had to go in and hold conferences with parents about their child's progress! It was nuts! Additionally, she was so sloppy in her haste to change grades that she forgot to alter the teacher comments. As a result, there were students with all A's and B's who had printed comments that indicated they were at risk for possible retention (kind of funny not funny)! I found myself in a quite a pickle (to say the least) but I wasn't going to put up a front as though everything was just fine (because that's what they wanted me to do) when it wasn't. God always provides a way of escape and this was no exception. I ended up using student performance on the district interim assessments to give parents a more accurate reflection of where their children were. It was uncomfortable but I got through it.

Not only was staffing the first grade class a challenge, but providing support for that class was also a challenge. There were very little teaching and student resources that were available for First Grade (as with other grades as well). Neither the teacher or student book sets in the Reading/Language Arts series were complete and what was perhaps worse was that those that were available didn't correspond with one another so they were worthless when considering their intended use. Although Ms. P was planning alongside the other first grade teacher who also lacked a complete set, it simply wasn't enough. As a teacher in high-poverty urban schools, especially my first couple of years, I often found myself with slim to no district-provided resources. I had to use some good ole' fashioned ingenuity and make do with what I had. The difference, however, is that all first-year teachers simply don't have the knowledge or capacity to pull it off. To be fair, that first year of teaching at any school naturally comes with its own set of difficulties for new teachers. You've got to study the curriculum and with every lesson strategize about how to make it work for your particular group of students, learn how to manage your classroom effectively, keep your students engaged, communicate with parents, keep tedious records for district and state compliance, and learn how to navigate the system. All of that and much more must be done on top of being mommy, nurse, counsellor, and teacher for each and every one of your students. Through trial and error, it typically gets better with each year of teaching but it certainly doesn't happen overnight.

Good teachers eventually learn how to anticipate certain difficulties before they arise so that they are better able to plan for them but it does take time. The very least we could do is set them up for success by providing (at minimum) the resources they need to implement the curriculum effectively but, apparently, that was asking too much. Asking for books was asking too much. Each month, when opening invoices from publishing companies that demanded payment for unpaid balances from previous years, I was reminded of why it was asking too much [insert sarcastic side eye followed by an eye roll here].

Loyalty

We were required to attend a district-wide retreat in Columbus for 2.5 days. Accommodations were made for two nights and all faculty and staff were to leave after school on a Wednesday and carpool the 2-hour drive to the hotel. There was an optional buffet and "meet and greet" later that evening and then the work day officially began the next morning. Middle school teachers were to attend a separate conference downtown during the day for the duration of the trip. Early childhood teachers were to attend a Math session on the first day (taught by an outside consultant) and then a Reading session on the second day which was thrown on me to lead and prepare for at the last minute (meaning, the day that we arrived). This "retreat", which had been characterized by the other administrators and superintendents as "a time to relax and have fun", had become anything but that for me.

    I attended the Math session with the early childhood teachers but in a working-on-my-PowerPoint-in-the-back-of-the-room sort of way. I tried to get an hour of "me time" in afterward so I didn't completely lose my introverted mind from being in "work mode" with "work people" around the clock for nearly 72 hours. I definitely have a people limit! Retail therapy away from the hotel appeared to be my best option, so I ventured out to do a little shopping. Unfortunately, my peace was disrupted shortly after I got to the store upon receiving a phone call from the Assistant Superintendent and the owner, Ms. Coin. Earlier that day, we (the principals) had been asked to submit the names of teachers and/or staff members who we felt had gone "above and beyond" for us. I had submitted my list and it was apparent that Ms. Coin had a problem with it. She went through each name that I listed and asked me to tell her why each name was on my list which, of course, I had no problem doing. These were people who stayed late planning with me, volunteered their time to work on special projects, and were eager to support both me and our students in any capacity. Her problem, however, was that her "favorites" didn't make the list but, of course, she indirectly communicated that. She inquired about specific teachers whom they had "always recognized". My response was that their work ethic had been average at best and a couple of them exhibited blatant defiance when it came to implementing new initiatives which would have had a direct, positive impact on our students. She concluded the conversation by informing me that she would look over the list again and make some final decisions before the certificates were prepared for the awards banquet later that evening.

I was more than pissed! How could a woman who had not stepped foot in our building all year make a valid decision about who had gone above and beyond for ME and our students? It was disrespectful to not only myself but the teachers who actually put in the work. Maybe in the past her beloved teachers were indeed a support but, for me, they had been more of a hindrance than anything else. Naturally, the change in leadership (after 10+ years) yielded some pushback from returning faculty and staff (which were very few) who may have been asked to try a different approach to doing some things that they had always done a certain way. Our school's current "F" status should have been enough indication that the school could benefit from some changes, but because change meant that her "loyal" teachers had to move out of their comfort zones and rethink ways of doing things, change wasn't welcomed, from the top down.

The awards banquet was the icing on the cake (no pun intended). It's intended purpose was to show appreciation for faculty and staff and to provide an opportunity for us to come together as a district and fellowship, but it certainly didn't feel like that. I reluctantly had to sit at the head table with district and school administrators (as opposed to sitting with my staff—which I would have preferred after being disrespected just hours earlier). We all sat and listened to Ms. Coin recap the history of the organization (eye roll) and reminisce about its golden days. Aside from her voice sounding like nails on a chalkboard as I listened in disgust, the irony of her braggadocios commentary made it far too interesting to simply tune her out. For example, at one point, she referenced wanting to take a trip to Africa and donate books.

One quick glance around the room after that remark captured unimpressed, stale, and bewildered expressions from teachers who were wondering when the woman was going to "donate books" to students in her own damn schools! Once her performance was over, she invited the "head table" to get food from the buffet table first. My immediate thought was, "way to show appreciation for your teachers whom we came to show appreciation for!" As much as I love food, I didn't want to move. It felt wrong and the look on my face must've communicated that plainly. It was at that moment that the Assistant Superintendent (whom I used to call friend) leaned over to me and said, "when in Rome, do as the Romans". I knew right then that we were cut from a very different cloth. God made me who I am, to be who I am in terms of my governing principles whether I'm in Rome or not.

Next came the awards and acknowledgements. Faculty and staff were acknowledged for years of service to the organization, high performance, and, in some cases, even low to modest performance (like aren't students SUPPOSED to show at least 7 months gain in a given school year?). Of course, some of the names I submitted for recognition were conveniently omitted while others I did not recommend were honored. It was truly a slap in the face, and I had to sit and endure the foolishness and blatant disrespect as it unfolded right in front of me. In that moment, I gained new insight about the people I worked for. It became obvious that company loyalty always overrides quality of performance. It didn't matter that our students' success or failure could depend on it. After the ceremony, I tapped out for an hour or so before returning to the lobby to fellowship with my teachers. The rest of the administration had retreated to the owner's suite for drinks and refreshments. Despite the turbulence of the day's events, I ended up having a great time bonding with faculty and staff over wine, card games, and a late-night visit to Waffle House.

Dirty Laundry Money

I had never seen our school budget and, as principal, that is extremely rare. Managing the budget for the building is typically a major part of any principal's role. From the start, however, it was clear that was not a responsibility that was designated to me (or any of our district's principals). If we needed funds to cover any costs in the building, I had to request them (translation: beg for them) from district office. Even the money we collected for our students to be able to dress down on Dress Down Days had to be sent out of the building to district office and then requested if needed. This obviously made it difficult to meet building needs as they arose and it frequently resulted in myself or my staff reaching into our own pockets to make purchases because we knew it would never get done otherwise. They would sit on purchase requests for weeks at a time with no explanation. Basic operating needs like having stamps for mailing letters home to parents were not provided. Anything that needed to be mailed had to be sent to the district office (by way of any of us who happened to be making that 45-minute commute) first and then they would mail it out.

Our lack of discretionary building funds resulted in much more than occasional inconveniences. I was particularly disturbed by what I had learned from our custodians. I had met with them to touch base regarding any maintenance concerns around the building. What they shared was appalling. Since we didn't have our own washer and dryer, all rags and mop heads used to keep the facility clean had to be taken to a Laundromat to be cleaned. The problem, however, was that the district hadn't been providing the money needed to purchase detergent or pay for the items to be washed. Recognizing the need, our nearly 80-year-old secretary had been giving our custodian the money needed to wash and, because of that, she was unable to wash as frequently as she should have been. Of course, she was concerned about the potential for cross-contamination when using the rags because access to clean rags was always limited. After I picked my jaw up off the floor, I let her know that was to stop immediately. I emailed the Superintendent right away to share my concern (because this sort of thing requires a paper trail), along with the laundry list (no pun intended) of other custodial concerns. Some of those concerns included the need for a new vacuum (the 20-year-old one we did have was broken down more than it ever worked), there was no dust mop for the gym (which made it difficult to keep the floor clean), and we needed a maintenance person on-site to deal with needs as they arose (every time we had something that needed to be fixed, which was often, we had to wait for them to send one of the two district maintenance personnel from the other locations that were 45 minutes away).

  Her response was astonishing. She told me that she was going to send cash with the maintenance man so that the rags and mop heads could be washed. She sent $10. You heard me right. Ten dollars. I thanked her for the $10 but kindly let her know that it wasn't enough money to purchase detergent and pay for the wash and dry cycles. In her final response, she directed me to take $5 from the dress down money we had recently collected to purchase detergent. Five dollars for a total of $15 to wash and dry rags and mop heads for the building that had not been washed in weeks. Need I say more. After all, we weren't talking about a large sum of money to purchase more of something we don't need; we were talking about money to cover BASIC OPERATING EXPENSES for the type of work that we did. No employee should be expected to cover the cost, and especially when you know they're already being underpaid. In this case, the need was urgent. Our ability to keep the building sanitary, as required by law, for the health and safety of our students was in jeopardy but it didn't matter to them and it hadn't mattered to them up until I demanded otherwise.

As the weeks progressed and I learned more about the people I worked for, I grew more and more outraged. When it came to resources in general, we were at the bottom of the barrel. The building was ancient and falling apart with cooling and heating issues that, at times, made it unbearable. When the air conditioners and fans were on at the same time, a fuse would blow. The heaters decided on their own when they would work and when they did you couldn't control the temperature. The drinking fountains and toilets were constantly breaking down. The fire panel would randomly beep for long periods of time because it needed to be serviced. Although many of those problems were fixable, it was obvious that the owner was not willing to invest any money into fixing anything. She had developed a reputation as a slum lord and rightfully so. It was especially upsetting to me because she owned the building outright and, therefore, didn't officially have building rent to pay (although she made sure she paid herself rent from our school's state funds anyway) but was still unwilling to do the right thing for the students whom her company was supposed to serve.

In terms of resources for our students, such as up to date technology and textbooks, our school was a far cry from what it could have been. We were fortunate enough to have 2 laptop carts with old laptops and internet access (whether or not they all worked half of the time was another story). One set was set up in our makeshift computer lab while the laptops from the other cart were distributed to the teachers so that they could have a couple computers in their classrooms for the children to use. There were two mobile Smartboards in the building and only one of them worked, sometimes. Projectors were a hot commodity, even the old-school ones with the transparencies and markers. There weren't enough to go around so the teachers made due and shared among each other. In terms of books, it was a constant struggle for teachers. The district didn't give us complete sets of pretty much anything so, when teachers tried to use the textbooks according to our pacing documents, they became frustrated. For example, a teacher might have the teacher text but the corresponding student storybooks would be missing. Some things I could anticipate, so I placed orders for them during the summer but the problem, however, was that the purchase orders sat at district office with no action taken. Every time I went to a meeting and inquired about the materials I got the same response, "we're working on it". Summer and Fall had come and gone and they were still "working on it". I ended up purchasing some of the books and other materials myself just so the teachers would have something to work with.

The mandatory board meetings that I attended sickened me. It was there that I discovered how the company itself worked. It was the only time that we (the principals) were given access to any form of financial records for our buildings. While they were talking, I would be studying the records. What I noticed, however, was that even though our income was itemized, our actual school expenses (salary payments, other bills, etc.) weren't reported in the books. The only line item that supposedly reflected our expenses was payment to Crooks Institute to "manage our resources". Managing our resources was supposed to mean paying all the bills on behalf of the school, but I knew that wasn't happening entirely. As I mentioned before, every month I would receive handfuls of unpaid invoices in the school mail. In addition, companies who offered services we needed, such as the alarm company and pest control, refused to do business with us at all unless unpaid balances were paid and future invoices were paid in advance or at the time of service. The only way for any of us to really know just how much of that money went toward actual school expenses would be if we had access to Crooks Institute financial records which, of course, we would not because it's a private company that is separate from the nonprofit (the schools). Crooks Institute is also owned by the same person who owns our building and founded our school district, the aforementioned slum lord, Ms. Coin.

At one of the board meetings, however, one hairline fracture created a leaky glass and it was obvious that Ms. Coin wasn't ready for it. None of us were. A gentleman from one of the area educational services centers showed up to the meeting and was recognized as a guest. It was understood that he was going to share something with the board that would be beneficial for our school district. He sat quietly and listened until it was his turn to have the floor. It was then that he revealed who he was and what he came for. As it turned out, our district owed the educational services center nearly $30,000 for special education related services that their employees rendered to students on our behalf (for things like speech therapy, etc). The man was extremely upset and he made it clear that those services would no longer be provided unless they were paid. He said that they had called, sent invoices and letters, and never received payment or a response. For the next couple minutes that followed, the room was so quiet that you could hear a pin drop. I know that those of us on my side of the table were shocked that he was bold enough to come in and do what he did and that he did it so smoothly. By law, Ms. Coin isn't supposed to speak at the meetings but she did that night, fumbling to muster up a rationale for lack of payment and response. After all he said he had done to get a response, the woman still pretended to be unaware of what he was talking about and insisted that payment was made.

At most, she was embarrassed and angry that he had the audacity to come it to HER meeting and do that but, beyond that, it didn't matter because HER board was in her pocket. They made a motion and moved to look into it and he left. Then they made motion and moved to continue to receive their stipend as board members which cost the district a total of $18,000 per year (and I was told by a colleague that they used to pay a whole lot more plus travel expenses). Do tell, how can a small, "struggling" district (what they would like to publicly portray) afford to set $18,000 aside to pay the board if they don't have enough money to pay necessary operating costs and secure proper resources for the students that they are supposed to be serving? It was approved and nobody blinked an eye. I guess the better question raised would be, "how can they afford to keep up the charades and not pay these people?" It was the only way her company could continue to do whatever it wanted without proper checks and balances from a legitimate board. Maybe the previous board meetings that took place before I came along were different. But, in those that I did attend, these people literally questioned nothing brought to the table. They just approved whatever was presented and any changes they were asked to approve. It was the ideal cover for a shady operation. You know, if there was one. I wondered what else they got in return, under the table.

Chartering False Hopes

Like other charter schools, Crooks Academy had so much potential. It had the potential to offer a viable alternative to the public school system, one that would give the city's most vulnerable population a chance to grow, thrive, and exceed their highest potential in a climate that respected and valued them. It had potential but it drastically missed the mark and it didn't have to. It was nothing short of an opportunity and resource desert disguised and presented as an oasis for our children. Once I realized that the people I worked for could really care less about creating this "private school experience in a public school setting" for our students (an experience they had convinced parents that they would provide), that the vision and mission of the organization amounted to nothing more than words on a page, I knew it was time for me to go. I didn't sign up to become part of another dog and pony show. I'd actually thought I was in a position to make a real impact until it become apparent that I was to be nothing more than a puppet and a politician, who was to smile, look pretty, and convince parents to keep sending their children—their most prized possessions, to a place that would never measure up to that which they deserved. Not because it couldn't measure up, but because it costs to measure up and businesses in the business of schooling (as with any other business) do everything possible to keep costs low and profits high. I couldn't do it. Not at the expense of children, mine included. What's more, in this case, it was us doing this to us. A Black company, sponsored by the state of Ohio, robbing Black and Brown children of their potential in effort to preserve personal gain. I later found out, Crooks Academy and Crooks Institute had been under investigation for years. They had even been sued by the state for mismanagement of funds, yet the school doors are still open. What more does it take? Not all charter schools are bad, but it's schools like these that make the Republican agenda for privatizing education a difficult pill to swallow.

Public schools are not holistically bad for all children, but when you start asking questions like, "for whose children?" then they're not as promising either. We know that the nation's public education system is broken but, with some intentional restructuring, it CAN work for all children. With an intentional shifting of funds, it CAN work for all children. The problem isn't public education. The problem lies with the INTENT. A redistribution of funds, an increase of funds, and some careful restructuring for the 21st Century would do far better for America's children than a privatized potluck at the tax payers' expense.

PART TWO: THE MACHINE & ME

"The old order ends...when the enslaved, within themselves, bury the psychology of servitude."

Dr. Martin L. King, 1963

It took me what seemed like an eternity just to start writing this book. I couldn't seem to get anything out and onto the page. I kept going over my thoughts again and again trying to frame and reframe the general concept. This struggle stretched beyond simple writer's block. Initially, I had considered shaping the book into an academic text. There were other scholars that I had in mind with relevant citations who I thought would be my "go to" people when I began to break down each topic and make it my own. I still struggled though. I knew that, no matter what, I did not want this book to become so much of a dense, academic text that the average person couldn't just pick it up and read without being put off too much by citations, the format, or the vocabulary. Eventually, I decided that it was best to just start writing, without adhering to the formalities that I had been taught. I decided to ignore what I had been ingrained in my head during my doctoral program. I decided to relinquish objectivity along with the need to constantly use someone else's research to define my own reality, to tell my story. It didn't make sense to me to do that, yet it was so difficult to abandon what I had been taught. By this, I recognized the machine at work. I had been conditioned to believe that my perceptions weren't valid unless someone else had already confirmed it in other words and through research. Furthermore, there was something in me that made me feel as though maybe my writing, my contribution, my story, wasn't good enough to become a published work.

At 34, with an earned Ph.D., I battled with the imprint of the machine on my psyche. Me, the girl who set high goals and crushed every single one of them. The same girl who, by faith, managed to persevere through all of life's challenges with her head held high. Yes me, "woke" as I am. The residue from the machine still discretely coated the inner workings of my mind. Once I could acknowledge that, I had to make a conscious decision to fight back. I was fully aware of the workings of the machine all around me and certain of that which I directly experienced but I had to dig deep to deconstruct its inner workings on me. The result was freedom, outside of the box.

'ROUND WHERE I'M FROM

I was born and raised in a little city outside of Cincinnati, Ohio called Hamilton. As a small child, I lived in the 2nd Ward with my family, across the street from the church that we attended. Hamilton's 2nd and 4th Wards were predominately African-American communities wherein many of its inhabitants, like ourselves, were considered lower middle-class or poor. My brother and I were fortunate enough to be raised in a two-parent household. My dad was a school custodian turned first black firefighter in our city and my mom was a seamstress who also worked odds and ends jobs as needed but, for the most part, stayed home with my brother and me. They both worked extremely hard to make sure we always had everything we needed. My dad is Black and my mom is White. It wasn't as common to see interracial families back then, and there were only a few other biracial children in the neighborhood. While we would visit my mother's side of the family occasionally, we spent most of our time with my dad's.

When I was in the second grade, my parents decided to send us to a public school outside of our neighborhood. My brother kept getting into trouble with his peers, so they thought that switching schools might help alleviate some of his behaviors. From the moment I walked in that first day, I knew I was different. Generally speaking, I never had a problem making friends. It was just a different experience than what I was accustomed to. Transitioning from our neighborhood school where most people were Black or Brown like me to a place where everyone wasn't made me feel different. We stayed at that elementary school for two years before changing schools again. This time, we changed schools because we moved. We moved to the west side of town "where the white people lived". In those days, in many unspoken ways, when you got to move to the west side of town, you'd "made it", so to speak.

While our new house was by no means a glamorous house by today's standards, it represented middle-class housing quite well. It was a nice upgrade. I just missed being close to my friends, along with the warmth of feeling welcomed in our own neighborhood. After all, we were a close-knit community. Everybody knew everybody and we looked out for one another. In our new neighborhood that certainly wasn't the case, especially when we first moved in. People would ride by our house and yell racial slurs out of the window. I remember walking home from the store with my brother and, as we approached her house, one of our new neighbors who was out on her porch saw us coming, grabbed her purse, went in the house and quickly closed the door as we passed by. Like really, what were we going to do to her that made her so afraid? At that time we weren't even teenagers.

At our new school, my brother and I were once again the only children of color, outside of my friend and her family who were Vietnamese. There I felt like I had to work harder to "fit in". I remember the first time I was called *nigger* by a classmate. I was in the fourth grade. We were playing a game at recess and the boy got upset because I beat him and called me a "stupid nigger". While I was, of course, offended, it made me sad more than anything. It was a reminder that no matter what I did to fit in, no matter how many friends I had made, at the end of the day I was still just a nigger in the eyes of some of my peers.

Junior high school was much worse. Early on, I noticed the differential treatment toward my Black peers who were bused from the housing projects from treatment of my White peers who had attended school with me. There seemed to be this sense of entitlement among the White students, but I felt like it emanated from teachers and administrators. Some students belonged while others simply didn't. My inner circle of friends at school was White. We had come directly from the same elementary school and were in the same classes. In fact, the only opportunities I had to interact with other Black students was when passing between classes, in the cafeteria, or immediately after school before the buses left. I was enrolled in all honors classes and they were not. At the time, I didn't question WHY they weren't (at least verbally anyway) but I wondered why and there was this unspoken, underlying assumption amongst us all that maybe they just weren't smart enough, and that bothered me.

Those were the years where I began to speak out against what I felt was so wrong about how the teachers would talk to us and treat us. What made all the difference for me is that I had parents who would come to school at the drop of a dime to see about me and the adults in the building were fully aware of that fact. One sobering observation came at the end of my ninth-grade year. Both Spanish classes took a field trip to Don Pablos, a commercial Mexican Restaurant (which, now that I think about it, is somewhat disrespectful, go figure). While at the restaurant, somebody got a classic teenage bright idea: "Let's put some stuff in the teacher's drink when she's not looking." Now, that somebody was not me but I did participate. The teacher walked away from her seat, her glass was passed around the table, and just about everybody put a little something in there from whatever was on the table. A little salt, pepper, sugar, and even a little hot sauce from yours truly. Naturally, the plan was a fail. She had noticed that her drink had been tampered with and didn't drink it but when we got back to school, somebody had to pay. That somebody was me. My involvement most certainly did not outweigh the involvement of all the other students seated around the same table; it wasn't even my idea. Yet, somehow, I became the fall gal. The only Black girl on the field trip. I was both puzzled and hurt. I had never been subjected to disciplinary action at school, but they wanted to suspend me for this, me alone, and of all the students from the class that they brought in for questioning, just two people told the truth to my defense. I was crushed. Yet again, it became painfully clear that at the end of the day, to them, I was still just a "stupid nigger".

The following school year, I was reunited with my friends from the East side of town. Students from each of the three junior high schools combined to attend the district's only public high school and, especially after last year's betrayal, boy was I happy to see them. Socially, I ran with my Black friends. Yet, as was the case in junior high school, the Black students at Hamilton High were in the academically average or below average classes. There was only one other Black student that attended Honors classes with me and that was my best friend Toni. However, there were a few of us in my elective courses and, once I joined the DECA Marketing program my junior and senior years, my classroom experiences became more diverse. I still couldn't understand why there weren't more of us in the Honors program, especially since I remembered some students from Epic, our 6th grade "gifted" pilot program (I can't say for certain that any of us were in fact tested and qualified for gifted programming as we know it now but I know it definitely wasn't for everybody). One day a week, "gifted" students from each of the district's elementary schools were bused to a building downtown to participate in problem-solving activities. The participants in Epic were diverse because each neighborhood school was represented, and I distinctly remember working with some of the city's brightest students, many of whom looked like me and even they weren't in my classes.

It wasn't until after high school (when I began to study Education and learn more about our education system) that I could pinpoint what I had both witnessed and experienced. On the surface, our schools didn't appear to be that bad. They came with all the bells and whistles (in that day) because they served a city with a majority White population and pretty much all the children in the city attended their neighborhood schools, which then funneled into three junior high schools and one public high school for all. The schools looked good physically. They presented well in terms of written curriculum and provided resources, but for the district's Black and Brown students and even some poor Whites, it was an opportunity desert from junior high school up. Our students became involuntarily nestled into lower academic tracks and, simultaneously, guided toward vocational programming in lieu of college bound prerequisite courses. School, as such, essentially became a place where existing stereotypes were easily reinforced. I graduated high school in 1999 and yet, more than 15 years later, the dynamics are essentially the same.

Even though the city's demographics have since become increasingly more diverse, the virtually all White teacher workforce also remains the same. As principal at a charter school in the city, I was invited to attend an annual awards banquet. The entire school district, in addition to surrounding private and charter schools, was represented in one room and I was the only Black person present. While it most certainly made me uncomfortable, this sea of white came as no surprise to me (Disturbing? Yes. Surprising? No.). My hometown has long preserved its tradition of White on White education and White on Black educational devaluation. The district has always maintained less than a handful of Black teachers and slim to none serving in administrative roles. In this city, the "Good Ole' Boys" system had always been and still remains in full effect.

ABSENT A MENTOR

I gave birth to two babies while teaching full-time and working full-time on my Ph.D. with no semesters off. Time was always limited so I never went to conferences or wrote anything "extra" to get published. Truth is, I never really understood the importance, that is, until after I graduated. No one in my family had ever done what I did. My Master's degree was a huge feat in and of itself but a Ph.D.? A Ph.D. was unheard of. By the grace of God, I finished it and then life took an unanticipated turn for me. I thought that I would be able to jump right into higher ed. to teach and conduct research—research was my passion, but it wasn't that simple. As it turned out, most institutions wanted to see a track record of conference presentations and publications to even consider me for a faculty position. To think, I managed to matriculate through undergrad and graduate school and complete my Ph.D. program without any real guidance. Yes, I had an academic advisor who helped me map out my coursework, yet even still, I lacked general understanding of the process itself—details about the way things worked which weren't printed on any curriculum maps or course guides. I don't fault my advisor and I own my own responsibility for seeking out help, but you can't seek help if you're unaware that it should be sought in the first place! I honestly don't think that my advisor was aware of my lack of understanding. This was simply another example of the tacit knowledge that most people who journey down the same path are privy to from previous exposure to the process, from having close relatives in these professional spaces, from networking and working the system that has worked for them. Even if she knew I was the first one in my family to attempt this great feat, I'm not sure that she would have understood what that entailed, that a person of my educational caliber could be so vulnerable to systemic defeat absent a mentor.

As I grappled with my own feelings of professional defeat that ironically surfaced almost immediately following what was definitely one of my greatest accomplishments, Distinguished Eagles (DE) was birthed. I took all that frustrated me about my own educational experiences, what I found to be lacking through the course of my own development, and designed a structure for a nonprofit that would prevent other children of color from falling through the cracks. It's mission: To increase the capacity of children of color to excel academically, socially, and economically through mentoring, advocacy, education, service, and partnerships. I just kept thinking, "What if our children came through the gate with the benefit of a mentor, with advocates to fight for access to equitable educational opportunity, with the tacit knowledge about the system that other people often take for granted, with the personal and spiritual development that is nurtured through our service to others, AND the luxury of relationships that offer real-world experiences and exposure?" Ultimately, it could change the game forever for our children and their families, for our communities, for generations to come.

PART THREE: THE MACHINE

"Education not only has been and will continue to be contested, but it is central to the larger struggle over what kind of society and government we desire."

Hursh, 2006

UNVEILED

Experience has taught me that, in this country and in others around the world, not all people are valued. The value that we attribute to one another can be determined by examining our behaviors toward one another, interactions with one another, and how we care for one another. When this concept is applied to the inner workings of our education system, it becomes painfully obvious who is valued and who is not. I mean, regardless of what their issues are at home outside of school, shouldn't all children be entitled to a well-rounded educational experience with rigorous coursework? Shouldn't their schools and classrooms be clean, warm, and inviting? Shouldn't their schools be well stocked with books, materials, up-to-date technology, and other resources? Shouldn't their teachers be highly-qualified, well-educated, experienced, motivated, passionate about teaching, and compassionate? The reasonable response that most of us would give, especially when attributing the same value we attribute to our own children to the children I'm referencing in these hypothetical questions, is unequivocally "yes, absolutely". Yet, even a quick glance across our nation's schools demonstrates that this is not the case for a majority of Black and Brown children and children of the poor.

The most recent data set released by the U.S. Civil Rights Data Collection (2013-2014), the CRDC, revealed that Black and Brown students in this country are more likely to attend schools with higher concentrations of inexperienced teachers and they still have unequal access to Advanced Placement courses, courses with high-rigor (such as Calculus, Physics, Chemistry and Algebra II), and other accelerated courses/programs used in part to determine college and career readiness. For example, only 33% of high schools attended by predominately Black and Latino students offer Calculus, but it was offered by 67% of high schools with low Black and Latino student enrollment. Physics was offered by only 48% of predominately Black and Latino high schools but, at the same time, offered by 67% of predominately White schools. In U.S. schools that offer gifted and talented education programs, only 28% of Black and Latino students were actually enrolled in those programs, even though they represented 42% of the total student body. Meanwhile, even though White student representation in schools that offered gifted programs was only 49%, 57% of them were admitted to those programs. In sum, rigorous, higher-level courses and gifted programs aren't even offered in over half of US public schools serving mostly Black and Brown children and, wherever such courses and programs are offered, Black and Brown students are disproportionately enrolled.

When it comes to school discipline in U.S. public schools, Black and Brown students are always subjected to school discipline measures far more than Whites, even in preschool. CRDC data (2013-2014) indicated that Black preschool children are 3.6 times as likely to receive one or more out-of-school suspensions as their white counterparts. In K-12 schools, Black students are 3.8 times as likely to be suspended. When compared to their White classmates, Black students in general are 1.9 times as likely to be expelled from school without educational services (CRDC, 2013-2014).

The current condition of the U.S. public education system, especially as it relates to minorities and children of the poor, is not accidental. This idea of the machine represents the arguably intentional, systemic negligence faced by Black and Brown people at large that is based upon an underlying assumption that Black and Brown people are not valuable, contributing members of society. It is the perpetuation of that assumption which secures the status quo, thus maintaining wealth for the wealthy, preserving precious feelings of White superiority, while reducing the likelihood of oppressed populations rising to power. Although my work primarily exposes the machine from within our country's education system, its reach extends far beyond it into all facets of our society, including our economic, justice, housing, and healthcare systems. By design, our nation's education system has laid the groundwork for maintaining the status quo in all areas. Even though state and national policies use attractive rhetoric to mask obscurities regarding equity, the fact is they still remain. Brown (1975) defined politics as "the art of allocating resources." He asserted that "nothing is more political than education" and that "it is through education that individuals are screened to share in the wealth of this nation…[and] whether minorities realize it or not, when they seek quality education they are asking for social, psychological, and economic equality as well, and such demands are wholly political." Where do the core problems of our education system lie? Politics. Education is dangerously political.

When DeVos was confirmed by the Republican regime as the new Secretary of Education by the 45th president, there was an outcry amongst educators who essentially declared that public education had just died. Indeed, it was painfully obvious that this woman is one of the most underqualified and unknowledgeable individuals to have been handed that role (or, to have purchased that role—whichever way you'd like to look at it). Subsequently, our public school system is likely to face an unprecedented amount of challenges now and in the years that follow but it didn't die with her confirmation. What should have died, however, was the general notion that public schooling was ever truly about educating ALL children in this country. In the past, the Republican agenda for education was masked in their irresponsible policy decisions disguised as attempts to help every child succeed (No Child Left Behind, etc.) and their fragile rationales for continuously keeping it underfunded. The general (uninformed) public could then at least try to maintain the assumption that everyone ultimately wants what's best for children. Now, the cards are lying face up on the table, unveiled for the world to see. I pray we're paying attention.

A DREAM DEFERRED: EVERY CLOSED EYE AIN'T SLEEP

Dr. Martin Luther King is most widely known for his role as a great leader in the African-American Civil Rights Movement. An activist who, like Mahatma Ghandi, was heralded for promoting the use of methods of nonviolent resistance in the quest for justice and peace which, in turn, helped garner the support of people all over the world. The, now iconic, *I Have a Dream* speech has since become the hallmark of Dr. King's work and is perhaps the only piece of his work that is promoted year after year as we celebrate him on his day. In several of his less widely-discussed writings, his words paint a strikingly different picture than what is often portrayed. Contrary to popular belief, Dr. King wasn't just some preacher with a lofty vision or a grand mouthpiece for peace without substantial action. You see, in his day, Dr. King was viewed as a radical. His actual message was radical. He spoke truth to power during a time when fear, acquiescence, and complacency crippled most others from doing so. He spoke out about issues that negatively impacted the human experience, such as racial injustice, poverty, and his opposition to U.S. presence in the Vietnam War. Hence, why we should find it not surprising that he was eventually assassinated. Dr. King was a prolific writer and orator who composed many brilliant works in which, nearly 50 years after his death, are just as relevant even now as they were back then.

I'd like to declare that today we have found ourselves amid a curious revolution. One marked by a collision of history and modern thought, silence and glaring frustrations, confusion and monumental clarity. The conscience of a people and a general public who had been strategically lulled to sleep appear to be engaged in the likes of a great awakening. Across this country, there have been people protesting; Black and White, rich and poor, people of all races, ages, and religions who have come together in solidarity. People who have come to realize that even now, there are systems in place which, as in the past, condone unequal treatment and violence against citizens of color in this country. America has, once again, figuratively found herself face to face with the large elephant that truly never left the room—racism. You see, until now, the concept of racism and use of the term had become somewhat taboo. It is certainly not a subject that people like to discuss. In some settings, the mere mention of the word causes some of us to feel uncomfortable.

While those of us who have lived with its presence and experienced its pain can understand this evil truth, there are yet people who refuse to admit it still exists. They want to know why black people are, in their view, always playing the "race card". They say that slavery and racism are a thing of the past and we should just move on. "Aren't you aware that our President was black?" You know these people. They make comments like: "The black men you are defending aren't victims of police brutality, they are criminals, thugs, who provoked the use of deadly force. Look at them, they murder one another and choose to engage in criminal activity. They don't care about education or meaningful employment, they chose government housing, welfare, and hustling. They chose to destroy their own communities with drugs and violence." You know these people. If you didn't before, chances are you probably do now.

It is true. Explicit Jim Crow laws which forbade African-Americans from using the same public facilities no longer exist. It is true. There are no explicit laws that forbid Black children from attending the same schools as their White counterparts or laws that explicitly forbid them from obtaining higher-level jobs in this country. It is true, we even had a Black President who happened to serve a second term. On the surface, one might conclude that the version of Dr. King's dream we've all been taught has been fulfilled; that sons of former slaves and sons of former slave-owners are now able to sit down together at the table of brotherhood, that our children are not judged by the color of their skin, that we can finally declare we are "free at last." On the surface, it appears that Dr. King's dream, which mainstream media has conveniently watered down and reduced to some cheap mythological trip down memory lane, to some now appears that the dream has been fulfilled. But, wake up! It's a dream deferred and every closed eye ain't sleep. The machine is at work. This is a curious revolution.

Vestiges of our past are both deliberately and systematically still present with us today. Covert forms of racism and white supremacy have replaced most of the outdated, explicit versions. Racism is fancy now. It seldom runs rampant in white sheets anymore. It's now hidden in plain uniforms—I mean plain sight, in the form of policies that have indirect, negative impacts on our communities at disproportionate rates; in tracking systems, and unfair hiring practices. You will find that integrated schools, like the ones where I'm from, remain segregated from within by race and class. I noticed that some districts even got creative with the labeling of their tracking systems now, where the "average" classes are called "collegiate" courses—misleading parents and their children by implying that these academically average courses prepare students for rigorous 4 year colleges and universities. The lowest of the three levels of classes, called "community-technical" courses, are said to prepare students for community college degrees and career technical training. Lately, they've done such a wonderful job preparing students that it often takes them 4yrs to earn a 2yr degree because many of those very students end up spending the first 2yrs of college taking classes designed for remediation, to prepare them for college course work. I'm quite sure you can guess what level of classes the majority of Black and Brown children and children of the poor have been assigned to. This concept is not new. Researchers have proven time and again that "curriculum tracks are generally color-coded, with advanced or honors level courses primarily reserved for White students, while the basic, remedial, or vocational tracks are disproportionately filled with children of color" (Darling-Hammond, p.52). Hence, opportunities for learning are not the same. Leading to opportunities for attending college and/or obtaining lucrative jobs after school that are also not the same. This feeds into the disproportionate numbers of our children who drop out or graduate but resort to selling drugs which, in turn, works to supply the prison-industrial-complex with enough free labor to run Massa's modern day plantations. The cycle simply continues. The machine is a work. This is a curious revolution.

We must not underestimate the critical role that our schools play in shaping the society in which we live. Our youngest, most vulnerable citizens are filtered through the conditioning system we call school. Dr. King (1958) declared that the ultimate tragedy of segregation is that it injures one spiritually, scars the soul, and degrades the personality. These children of color who are segregated are inflicted with "a false sense of inferiority," while their white and upper class counterparts gain a "false estimate" of their "own superiority." That system "forever stares [our children] in the face, saying: You are less than…You are not equal to" (p.37). Unknowingly, we are left with a compromised self-worth that has been subjected to the manipulation of system that was never designed to give us an equal chance. Our children then come to believe that they will never be as smart as their White peers—that they will never be good enough so they accept less and come to expect less. Then we have the audacity to turn our noses up at our young people who have come to equate the academic successes of their peers with "acting white". We may not like to admit it or may simply not be aware that the scars from this institutionalized conditioning live with us all today. That's why, unlike people of other cultures, many of us that "make it" don't hire or do business with other people who look like us. The reverse is also true. In the process, students of the dominant culture are conditioned to believe that Black and Brown people are inferior, that they aren't as smart or good enough. Subconsciously, the status quo is automatically reinforced. The machine is at work. This is a curious revolution.

In 1962, Dr. King spoke about the planned and institutionalized racism that he brilliantly dubbed as "tokenism" (aka "token integration"). He pointed to the fact that our country had "advanced in some places from all-out, unrestrained resistance, to a sophisticated form of delaying tactics embodied in tokenism." This, he identified as "one of the most difficult problems that the integration movement confronts" (King, 1962, p.107). Just as a person can be handed a token as a symbol that holds some predetermined value, African-Americans were handed a token that awarded equal rights and access to equal educational opportunities in this country. Tokenism…

> "meant that Negroes could be handed the glitter of metal symbolizing the true coin and authorizing a short-term trip toward democracy. But he who sells you the token instead of the coin always retains the power to revoke its worth…Tokenism is a promise to pay. Democracy, in its finest sense, is payment…schools, jobs, housing, voting rights and political positions—in each of these areas,

manipulation with tokenism was the rule. Negroes had begun to feel that a policy was crystalizing--- all their struggles had brought them merely to a new level in which a selected few would become educated, honored and integrated to represent a substitute for the many" (King, 1963, p.17).

While Dr. King was referring to the manipulation of African-Americans over fifty years ago, it undeniably bears a striking resemblance to the happenings of today. These modern day color-blind notions serve to endorse the tokenism that has historically permeated the plight of African-Americans and other minorities. They create the illusion that somehow racism, discrimination, and segregation are no longer problems in this country which, in turn, threatens the validity of such claims, making it increasingly more difficulty to come together and discuss possible solutions for such problems. In other words, folk can point to our Black President and say "see, people are color-blind; we elected a Black President." Even though they fought him tooth and nail at every turn. He was always the exception, never the rule. People can point to the one black lady, deliberately planted as the face of Human Resources in Hamilton, and say "see, this city hires Black employees; we're not the problem, they just don't apply." They can point to Dr. Sutton and say "see, our school system isn't bent in favor of upper class Whites, she was able to successfully make it through and even obtain her Ph.D." Even though the only reason I wasn't filtered into the lower academic tracks was likely because I attended a predominately White elementary school and my grades were impeccable so they skipped over me while they funneled my gifted Black friends and family from the predominately Black schools directly into the lower tracks. I was always the exception, never the rule. When applying such color-blind notions in a country so drenched in racist ideology, there exists the ability to dismiss the unnerving statistics and overwhelming amount of evidence and research which so lucidly demonstrate that the token was indeed null and void. The machine is at work.

This professed color-blindness and the promotion of racially neutral policies that, for the past two decades now, have been overturning legislation that people like Dr. King have fought to secure, only work together to solidify a barrier to dealing with our nation's problem of race. As one pair of scholars explained, when "color-blind" law is used to equate "White identity" to all other group identities, "Whiteness," which is based on privilege and racial exclusion, can be denied. As a result, white privilege that has been historically accumulated, coupled with the status and property that white privilege secures, is protected" (William & Spriggs, 1999). The machine is at work. This is a curious revolution.

In his 1958 text entitled *Stride Toward Freedom*, Dr. King presented some of the tangled challenges they faced in their quest for justice. He noted that the masses accepted segregation and the abuses, and indignities which came with it, without protest. They chose to acquiesce. In their acquiescence, the oppressed chose to "tacitly adjust themselves to oppression, thereby becoming conditioned to it" (p.211). Dr. King said that, "In every movement toward freedom, some of the oppressed prefer to remain oppressed" (p.211). But, "to accept passively an unjust system is to cooperate with that system, thereby the oppressed become as evil as the oppressor" (p.212). Did you know that your silence is consent?

Perhaps it is our own acquiescence then that has helped bring us to a place where the conscience of a nation has fallen asleep. Past generations saw the tokens, stopped fighting for justice, and set out to forge their own paths despite the broken system. As a people, we subsequently fell back and accepted the injustices we experienced to be "just the way it is for Black people living in America" in exchange for a fraction of economic security and advancement. Our silence on the presence of the institutionalized racism we've experienced has worked to secure its modern-day presence as a myth to those whose privilege keeps them insulated from its effects. The machine is at work. This is a curious revolution.

I have two Black boys, Dre who is 4 and Drew who is 7. Drew was reading fluently by his 4th birthday and Dre has also exceeded the academic expectations for children his age. As an educator and as a concerned parent, I often ponder the endless possibilities of their future and every ounce of me wants to do everything that I can to make sure they are well-prepared for life, for whatever it is that they endeavor to do. I want to make sure that I raise independent, critical thinkers who are socially and politically conscious, great problem-solvers who embrace challenges and work to overcome them, young men who are well-mannered, empathetic, and compassionate to all people. Yet, I cringe at the thought of sending them to school.

My two Black boys. Young and unguarded. Entering a system of deeply rooted structural inequalities for children who look like them. A system

I know all too well that does not favor nor does it breed the type of children that I described. My two Black boys. Who, in the minds of some who are charged to teach them, are deemed inherently inferior and incapable of achieving high-levels of academic success. My two Black boys. Who, in America, could be stalked and gunned down by a grown man while simply walking home from the store. My two Black boys. Who, in America, can't be seen buying or playing with toys in public without bolstering the unwarranted fear of those around who may perceive them as a threat. My two Black boys. Who, in America, can be college graduates but still labeled as thugs. My two Black boys. Who, in America, can be pulled over while driving and brutally beaten at the will of police officers without just cause. My two Black boys. Who, in America, can be fatally shot with their hands in the air while surrendering to a crime that they did not commit. My two Black boys. Who, in America, still have to fight for the basic human right to live. My two Black boys, born into system that places NO value on their lives and NEVER has. I raise the question: When is enough, enough?

When Dr. King delivered his last Sunday morning sermon at the National Cathedral in Washington, DC, he referenced a popular short story by Washington Irving entitled: *Rip Van Winkle*. As you may recall, Rip Van Winkle had gone up into the mountain to go hunting and while he was there, he met some explorers whom he ate and drank with then fell into a sudden, deep sleep. When he woke up from his sleep, he discovered that twenty years had passed by. When he went up into the mountain, the sign had a picture of King George III of England but when he came down there was a picture of George Washington. Dr. King stated that:

> "The most striking thing about the story of Rip Van Winkle is not merely that Rip slept twenty years, but that he slept through a revolution. While he was peacefully snoring up in the mountain a revolution was taking place, that at points would change the course of history—and Rip knew nothing about it: he was asleep.

Yes, he slept through a revolution. And one of the great liabilities of life is that all too many people find themselves living amid a great period of social change and yet they fail to develop the new attitudes, the new mental responses—that the new situation demands. They end up sleeping through a revolution (King, 1968 p.269)."

Are you STILL asleep today? I've come to realize that, as in the case with Dr. King, people don't have a problem with our dreams as long as we remain asleep. This is a curious revolution, not because it shouldn't be happening now, but because after a half of a century of self-sustaining silent struggling, this nation is finally waking up. Our people are rising up. Are you STILL asleep today? What is happening now is not a Ferguson issue; it's not a St. Louis, a Staten Island, a Cleveland, a Beavercreek or Cincinnati, Ohio issue—it's an American issue, and just because it may not appear to have arrived at our front door to the degree that it has someplace else yet doesn't mean that it doesn't exist. The machine is at work. Are you STILL asleep today? Dr. King (1958) proclaimed that, "there comes a time when people get tired of being trampled by oppression" and that time, my friends, is upon us (p.69). That time is right now. Are you STILL asleep today? I must say that I concur with Dr. King (1968) when he attested that "it may well be that we will have to repent in this generation. Not merely for the vitriolic words and the violent actions of the bad people, but for the appalling silence and indifference of the good people who sit around and say, wait on time" (p.270). The time is now.

I agree with Dr. King (1958) when he said, "True peace is not merely the absence of tension; it is the presence of justice" (p.40). The time is now. Let us come together to demand justice. The time is now. We will not remain asleep through this revolution. The time is now.

Afterword

It has been a little over a year since I left my job and my feeble, human mind simply could not have imagined life as I know it now. There are days that I wake up and I'm like, "Wait, what? I bake cakes for a living now?", and I just have to laugh at the often-puzzling works of the Lord. While I am especially proud of what I have accomplished as I reflect upon the journey, I must confess that it hasn't always been easy. I've had to work at least 5 times as hard to earn just a small fraction of what I made before. It was discouraging at times and I had to encourage myself by reminding myself how I got to this point in the first place. I was led to take a leap of faith outside of the comfort of economic stability and that's what I did. God taught me a long time ago that if He leads you into it, He'll personally guide you through it. Retaining my integrity was worth far more than maintaining a compromising position to earn a living.

God has been nothing short of faithful to His word. I started a business, Sugar (a home bakery that specializes in custom cakes and cupcakes), that I did not anticipate and I learned so much along the way. I preached my initial sermon and, for me, that was huge. Before I left my job, I had become borderline diabetic, mentally drained, and emotionally spent, but I'm much healthier now. I traveled to several countries that I hadn't been to before and, best of all, I was fortunate enough to spend more quality time with my young children. I'm left in awe at His grace and sufficiency. My goal for 2016 was to finish this book and allow God to lead me where He saw fit. I haven't arrived at that destination yet and I still can't quite see it, but I'm confident that I'm well on my way.

When God says move, move. Trust that, somehow, He has already worked it out. Every. Single. Thing. Freedom exists when we relinquish our fears. Find your freedom.

References

Ayers, W., Quinn, T., Stovall, D., & Scheiern, L. (2008). Teachers' experience of curriculum: Policy, pedagogy, and situation. In Connelly (Ed.). The Sage Handbook of Curriculum and Instruction, (pp.306-326). Thousand Oaks, CA: Sage.

Brown, F. (1975) Problems and Promises of Urban Public Schools. *The Journal of Negro Education.*

Darling-Hammond, L. (2010). The Flat World and Education. New York: Teacher's College Press.

Darling-Hammond, L. (1997). The right to learn: A blueprint for creating schools that work. San Francisco: Jossey-Bass.

Honig, M. I. (2009). What works in defining "what works" in educational improvement: Lessons from education policy implementation research, Directions for future research. In Sykes, G., Schneider, B. & Plank, D. (Eds.), Handbook of Education Policy Research, (pp.333-347). Thousand Oaks, CA: Sage.

Ingram, D., Louis, K. S., & Schroeder, R.G. (2004). Accountability policies and teacher decision making: Barriers to the use of data to improve practice. Teachers College Record, 106(6), 1258-1287.

King, M.L. (1968) Remaining Awake Through a Great Revolution in *A Testament of Hope*. New York: Harper One.

King, M.L. (1958) *Stride Toward Freedom*. New York: Harper & Row.

King, M.L. (1963) *Why we can't wait*. New York: Harper & Row.

Payne, C.M. (2010). So much reform, so little change. Cambridge, MA: Harvard Education Press.

Williams, R.M., Spriggs, W.E. (1999) How does it feel to be free?: Reflections on black-white economic inequality in the era of "color-blind" law. *The Review of Black Political Economy*.

www.ingramcontent.com/pod-product-compliance
Lightning Source LLC
Chambersburg PA
CBHW020910090426
42736CB00008B/572